Using Math in Science

by Kathy Furgang

Table of Contents

4 — **INTRODUCTION**
Math and Science in Our World Today
How much do we rely on math and science every day?

6 — **CHAPTER 1**
Measurement
How are quantities measured and described?

Cartoonist's Notebook 18

20 — **CHAPTER 2**
Mathematical Relationships
How can relationships between numbers be described and determined?

32 — **CHAPTER 3**
Representing and Interpreting Data
How can data be organized and interpreted?

42 — **CONCLUSION**
The World of Mathematics and Science Grows 42

How to Write an Objective Argument 44

Glossary 46

Index 48

INTRODUCTION

Math and Science in Our World Today

Think of what your life would be like without electricity. Now imagine a world with no modern transportation like cars or jet planes. What would it be like to not be able to watch television or listen to music? What if you weren't even able to keep track of time? It's easy to reach for your cell phone, video game, or computer without thinking about math and science. It's easy to check a clock for the time and get on with your day. But make no mistake—without math and science, none of these marvels of technology would exist.

Over the centuries, people slowly developed a system of mathematics. In time, they also gained the scientific knowledge that we take for granted today. They learned about the materials that make up life. They learned how to design and build an engine. They learned how to use chemicals to capture an image. They learned how to make a radio signal travel through the air and a plane fly through the sky. Their lives became easier with each scientific invention and discovery. One language made all of these developments possible.

That language is mathematics. It allows us to convey measurements, understand relationships in nature, and display and interpret data. Together, math and science have helped us cure deadly diseases and build rockets carrying astronauts into space. Math and science have provided pilots with the tools to land airplanes safely. Math and science have helped people measure the wind speed and temperature of a hurricane in order to make predictions and save lives.

Even our favorite kinds of entertainment use the language of math and science. Think about going to the movies. Science and math help capture and create the image of the film. Physics is involved in projecting a movie onto a large screen. Chemistry is even involved in making your popcorn taste just right!

We live in a world that allows us to enjoy the results of using math and science. We advance as a society because we understand math and science and are eager to learn what else they can teach us. Who knows what exciting discoveries math and science will bring us in the future? Whatever they may be, it's clear that the language of math is definitely worth learning!

▼ Each year, advances in math and science influence design and technology.

CHAPTER 1

Measurement

How are quantities measured and described?

In many ways, the languages of math and science are the same. Using measurements is one of the most important ways a scientist can express data. All experiments need to be repeated to show that the results can be duplicated. Numbers and quantities are extremely important for this to happen. Imagine trying to explain the results of your experiment to someone without the language of math. Your communication would be both difficult and inaccurate.

For centuries, units of measurement have allowed people to measure and calculate quantities. Quantitative data tell about amounts. Numbers are used to express quantitative data. For example, we use numbers when we talk about temperature or length. Any description that doesn't use numbers is qualitative. When we describe what something looks or feels like, we are using qualitative data. Scientists use both qualitative and quantitative descriptions in their studies.

The elegant Louvre Pyramid ▶ in Paris, France, is made of steel and glass. It was built between 1985 and 1989. The base is 35.42 meters (116 feet) wide. The height of the pyramid is 21.64 meters (71 feet) tall.

21.64 m

35.42 m

ESSENTIAL VOCABULARY
- customary system p. 8
- dimensional analysis p. 13
- estimate p. 16
- exponent p. 14
- formula p. 12
- metric system p. 9
- scientific notation p. 14

▲ Built between 1870 and 1883, the Brooklyn Bridge in New York is a remarkable achievement in engineering. As beautiful as it is sturdy, the total length is 6,827 feet (2,081 meters). The height of each tower is 268 feet (81.7 meters) above high water.

The magnificent Temple of ▶ Quetzalcoatl in Chichen Itza, Mexico, was built between 550 and 900 C.E. This massive stone structure is 24 meters (78.7 feet) in height, not including the 6-meter (19.7-foot) temple on top.

Chapter 1

The Customary System

A system of measurements was established centuries ago to help people understand one another when they talked about things such as length. An inch is roughly the width of a thumb, and a foot is named after that part of the body. A cubit was the term used to describe the length of a forearm. In the Roman Empire, a mile described about a thousand paces. People used these approximations to explain the distances between villages, the length of objects, and the measurements for building things. To describe weight, people compared things with the weight of wheat. For volume, they compared things with the volume of baskets, sacks, or pottery jars.

After a while, people realized that measurements could not be accurate if they were not standardized. Because people's thumbs can be many different widths, the length of an inch was never exactly the same. Therefore, the standard system of measurements was introduced. Once the length of an inch was standardized, a foot could be defined as 12 inches, a yard as 3 feet, and so on. Measurements became more accurate once the **customary system** was established. Still, different cultures and countries used different standardized units. And converting feet to inches, or pounds to ounces, involved a variety of coefficients.

BODY PARTS AND ANCIENT MEASUREMENT

Cubit
Ancient = from the elbow to the end of the fingertips
Today = 18 inches

Hand
Ancient = 5 digits
Today = 4 inches (horses are measured in hands)

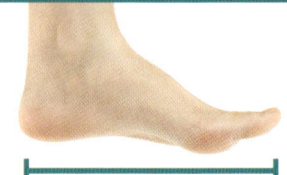
Foot
Ancient = 11 1/42 inches
Today = 12 inches

Yard
Ancient = distance from a man's nose to the end of his outstretched arm
Today = 36 inches

Mile
Ancient = 1,000 paces
Today = 5,280 feet

8

Quantity	SI Base Unit	Metric	Customary
length	meter (m)	millimeter (mm)	inch (in)
		centimeter (cm)	foot (ft)
		meter (m)	yard (yd)
		kilometer (km)	mile (mi)
mass	kilogram (kg)	gram (g)	n/a
		kilogram (kg)	n/a
weight	n/a		ounce (oz)
		newton (N)	pound (lb)
volume	n/a	milliliter (mL)	fluid ounce (fl oz)
		liter (L)	gallon (gal)
temperature	kelvin (K)	Celsius (°C)	Fahrenheit (°F)
time	second (s)	second (s)	second (s)

The Metric System

To avoid these problems, a new system of measurement was developed in the late 1700s. After France adopted the units in the 1800s, the **metric system** was soon accepted by other nations. The metric system is a standardized system of measurements based on multiples of 10. Using the number ten makes it unnecessary to do conversions like dividing by 16 to convert ounces to pounds or by 12 to convert inches to feet. More importantly, it based its measurements on fixed standards. For example, the standard unit of length was taken from a portion of Earth's circumference and was called the meter. The units for volume and mass were derived from this length. This made the basic units related to one another. Larger and smaller multiples of these units could be obtained simply by moving the decimal point to either the right or to the left. You can tell if a measurement is large or small by looking at the prefix in front of the unit. For example, a meter is a base metric unit of length. The prefix *milli-* means "one-thousandth." So a millimeter is one-thousandth of a meter. The prefix *centi-* means "one-hundredth." A centimeter is one-hundredth of a meter. On the other hand, the prefix *kilo-* means "one thousand." Therefore, a kilometer is one thousand meters.

As scientific advancement continued, the metric system underwent some fine-tuning. Soon new standards for length and mass were established. Finally in 1960, the General Conference on Weights and Measures adopted a revised system that used seven base units: the meter for length, the kilogram for mass, the second for time, the kelvin for temperature, and three others that were essential for chemists and physicists to share their research. In English, this system is called the International System of Units, abbreviated SI.

CHAPTER 1

HANDS-ON SCIENCE
Measuring Volume with Accuracy

MATERIALS

- 5 graduated cylinders ranging in size (10 mL, 25 mL, 50 mL, 100 mL, 250 mL)
- 25-mL beaker

TIME

45 minutes

PROCEDURE

1. Fill the beaker with water.
2. Transfer 5 mL of water from the beaker to a 250-mL graduated cylinder.
3. Then pour the 5 mL of water in the 250-mL graduated cylinder into a 10-mL graduated cylinder.
4. Carefully read and record the amount of water seen in the 10-mL graduated cylinder.
5. Repeat steps 1–3 three more times with the remaining graduated cylinders.
6. Compare the four final measurements recorded in step 4.

ANALYSIS

1. Describe how you would measure 15 mL of water needed for an experiment.
2. What general statement (rule) might you make about the laboratory equipment used in an experiment?

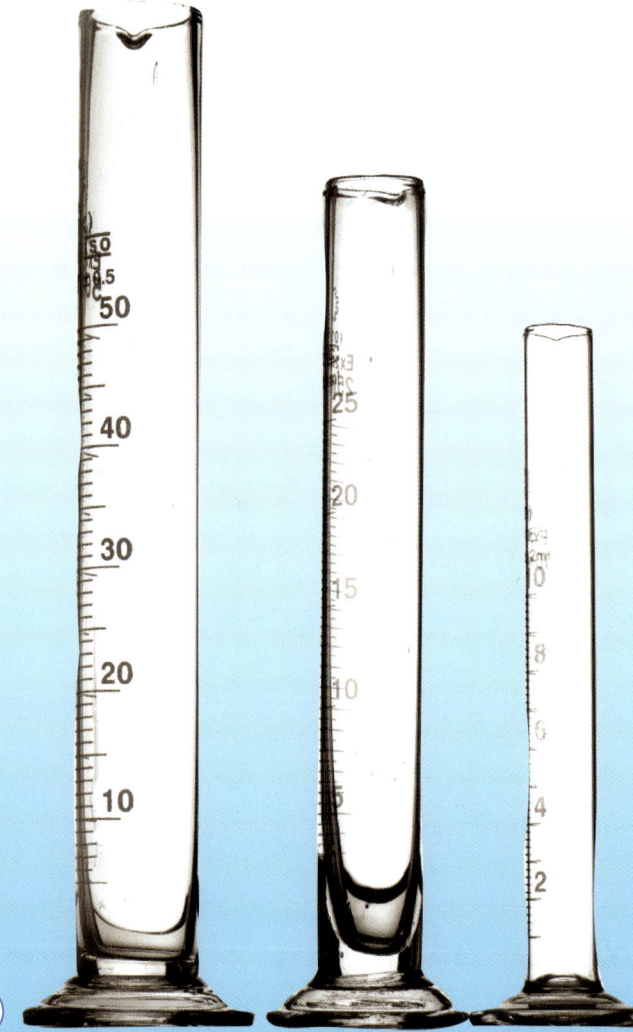

Length

Length tells how long something is. You will find centimeter and millimeter marks on a metric ruler or a meter stick. The closest metric unit to a mile is a kilometer, which is approximately six-tenths (6/10 or 0.6) of a mile.

Temperature

In the metric system, temperature is measured in degrees Celsius. The base SI unit for temperature is degrees kelvin, although scientists around the world also use degrees Celsius. On the Celsius thermometer, water freezes at 0° and boils at 100°.

Volume

Volume is the amount of space something takes up. A liter is the usual unit of volume in the metric system. A milliliter is equal to one-thousandth of a liter. Graduated cylinders are tools used to measure the volume of liquids. This type of cylinder has measurement marks running along its side.

Mass

Mass is the quantity of matter that an object has. A kilogram is the base, or standard unit of mass, in the metric system. A balance is used to measure mass. A paper clip is roughly a 1-gram unit. What do you think might have a mass of 1 kilogram, or 1,000 grams?

▼ **We can use a triple beam balance to measure mass.**

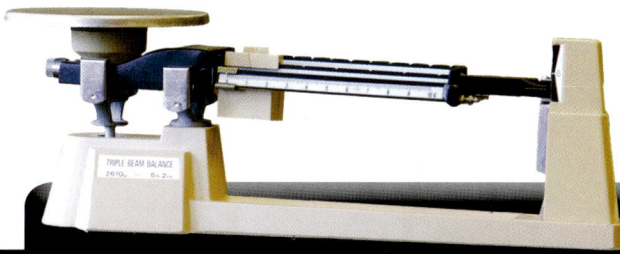

EVERYDAY SCIENCE

Mass vs. Weight

People often confuse the measurements of mass and weight. Mass is the amount of matter in an object. Weight is the measure of gravity's pull on that object. A balance tells the mass of an object, and a scale tells the weight of an object. To tell the difference, remember that your mass is always the same wherever you go. You have the same amount of matter in you. But if you go to the moon, your weight will be different because the pull of gravity on the moon is different from the pull of gravity on Earth.

CHAPTER 1

Derived Units

A derived unit is one that is found by using more than one measurement. If you travel 2 kilometers, your speed is not determined until you know how long it took you to travel the 2 kilometers. Speed is determined by dividing the distance traveled by the time elapsed. That is why we talk about speed in terms of kilometers per hour. A **formula** is a mathematical rule or relationship that is expressed in symbols. This formula is used to calculate speed:

$$s = \frac{d}{t}$$

$$\text{Speed} = \frac{\text{distance}}{\text{time}}$$

Volume can be a derived unit. We can use different formulas to find the volume of a three-dimensional shape. For example, to find the volume of a rectangular prism, you can multiply its length by its width and its height ($v = l \times w \times h$). Density is also a derived unit. It is found by dividing mass by volume. The formula used to find density is:

$$\text{Density} = \frac{\text{mass}}{\text{volume}} \qquad d = \frac{m}{v}$$

▼ The bike rider's speed can be found by dividing the distance traveled by the time it took to travel that distance.

SCIENCE AND TECHNOLOGY

Accuracy vs. Precision

What is the difference between measurements that are accurate and ones that are precise? These may sound very similar based on the dictionary definitions, but they are different in science. In science, measurements must be both accurate and precise in order for results and measurements to be repeated. When a measurement is accurate, it is correct. But does it mean that it is precise? A precise measurement is one that can be repeatedly determined with the same accuracy each time. You must repeat measurements many times to see if they are precise. You may find that the average of your measurements is accurate, but each individual measurement is off by a small amount. Repeating measurements to be sure they are both precise and accurate is an important part of science.

Checkpoint ✓

Talk It Over

The United States is one of the only countries in the world that uses the customary system of measurement. Europe, Asia, and the rest of the world use the metric system exclusively. Do you think the United States should convert to the metric system? Why or why not?

Unit Conversions

When you convert one unit to another, you are using a mathematical concept called **dimensional analysis**. This is the practice of expressing units that show the same relations between them. When you convert yards to inches, for example, you are not changing the length you are talking about. You are simply changing the unit used to measure them. You can use dimensional analysis in most types of measurement, such as time, volume, mass, and length.

Dimensional analysis works in both the customary and the metric systems. You can convert 500 milliliters to 1/2 liter, or 5 deciliters. If you know that there are 60 seconds in 1 minute and 60 minutes in 1 hour, you can use multiplication to find out how many seconds are in 24 hours.

Similarly, if 3 feet equal 1 yard, then you can use division to find out how many yards are in 108 feet.

You can even convert customary units to metric units or metric units to SI units. If you read a science experiment involving milliliters, you may want to find out how many ounces are involved. There are 29.5735296875 mL in one ounce. This kind of conversion is cumbersome to calculate, but many conversion tables are available to make the transferring easier. It is often helpful to round that number to 30 for easier calculations.

Most scientific rulers show metric units on one side and customary units on the other side. If you examine one of these rulers, you can see that there are 2.54 centimeters in one inch.

▲ Some rulers allow you to convert a customary unit to a metric unit without calculations.

CHAPTER 1

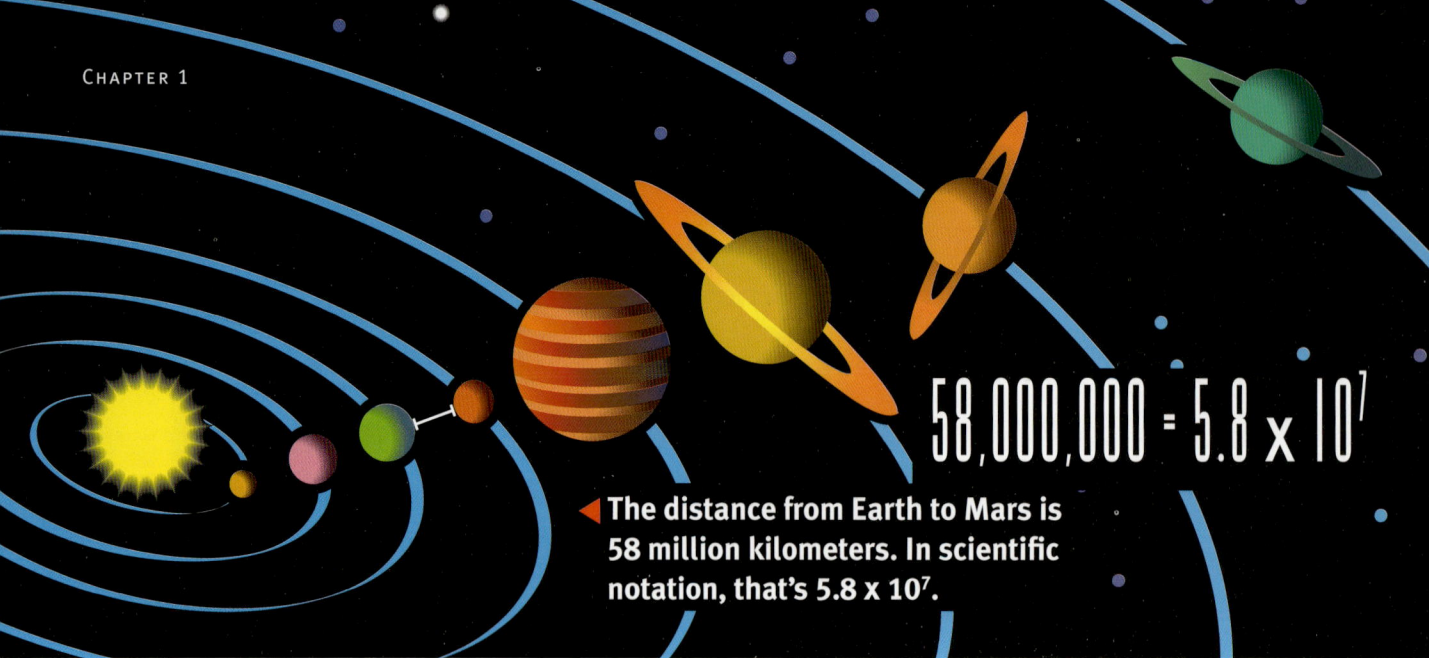

The distance from Earth to Mars is 58 million kilometers. In scientific notation, that's 5.8×10^7.

$58,000,000 = 5.8 \times 10^7$

Writing Numbers in Scientific Notation

Have you ever come across numbers that are too big or too small to write out conveniently in number form? For example, 4 trillion looks like this: 4,000,000,000,000. A more convenient way to write such a large number is to use **scientific notation**. This is a way of writing numbers in a decimal form by using exponents. An **exponent** is the power to which a number or expression should be raised. So 4 trillion in scientific notation is 4×10^{12}. It means 4 x 10 to the 12th power. Scientific notation works with decimals, too. If a number is too small to be expressed in numbers, such as one ten-thousandth, it might be easier to write the number in scientific notation, or 1×10^{-4}.

Scientific notation is used frequently to express numbers in science. It is convenient to indicate the size of a human cell, the age of a fossil, or the distance between Earth and a faraway planet.

Scientific notation may look difficult to read, but it follows a pattern. The chart on the opposite page shows how to represent numbers as decimals and how each number is shown in scientific notation.

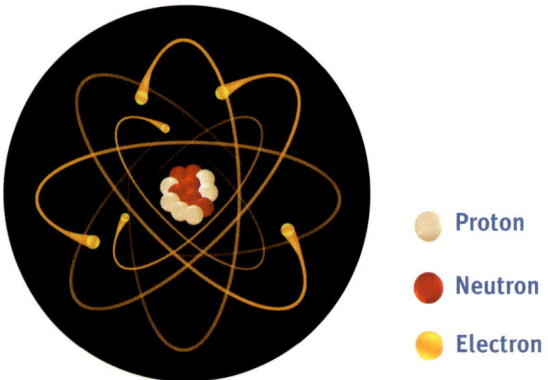

- Proton
- Neutron
- Electron

$m = 9.10938188 \times 10^{-31} \text{ kg}$

▲ The mass of an electron is 0.00000000000000000000000000000910938 kg. That is 9.10938×10^{-31} kg in scientific notation.

14

MEASUREMENT

SCIENCE AND MATH

Scientific Notation

A unit of measurement often used when describing atoms is a nanometer. One nanometer (nm) is one billionth of a meter. How many meters is 15 nanometers? Use scientific notation for your answer.

Number in Words	Decimal	Scientific Notation
one-thousandth	0.001	1×10^{-3}
one-hundredth	0.01	1×10^{-2}
one-tenth	0.1	1×10^{-1}
one	1	1×10^{0}
ten	10	1×10^{1}
one hundred	100	1×10^{2}
one thousand	1,000	1×10^{3}

▼ Scientists can date rocks and fossils back to the time they were formed. The oldest rock on the Earth's surface is more than 3,800,000,000 years old. That's 3.8 billion, or 3.8×10^{9} years old.

$$3,800,000,000 = 3.8 \times 10^{9}$$

Chapter 1

Estimation

When talking about very large or very small numbers, it is not always necessary to give exact numbers. Sometimes an **estimate** is good enough. An estimate is not exact, but it is close to the actual answer. For example, the speed of light is 299,792.458 kilometers/second (186,411.358 miles/second). You might round that number to about 300,000 kilometers (185,000 miles) per second. If you are doing a rough calculation, an estimate may be accurate enough. However, if you are doing an exact calculation, using an estimate would make your answer incorrect. You would have to use the exact measurement of 299,792.458 kilometers (186,411.358 miles) per second.

When doing an experiment, you might estimate the results of your testing to make communication easier and clearer. But the measurements you record and the calculations you make must be based on exact measurements.

Can you estimate the number ▶ of coins in this jar?

Summing Up

- Long ago, people established units and systems to measure length, mass, volume, temperature, and time in a consistent way.

- The customary system (inches, pounds, gallons, etc.) is the standardized system of units used in the United States.

- The metric system is based on multiples of ten. These standardized units (meters, liters, grams) are used in most countries around the world.

- We can express measurements in different units in the same system or convert back and forth between systems of measurement.

- Scientists use a universal system of measurement to share their research called the International System of Units (SI). The meter (length), the kilogram (mass), the second (time), and the kelvin (temperature) are among the seven universal or SI units.

- Derived quantities, such as speed and density, are calculated using formulas.

- Measurements can be expressed in shortened forms. They can also be expressed as estimates or exact numbers, depending on how they will be used.

Putting It All Together

Choose from the research activities below. Work independently, in pairs, or in small groups. Then share your findings with the class.

1 Throughout history, people have used a variety of units of measurement. In a group, research early or unusual units of measurement, such as units of barley or salt. Present your findings in a poster.

2 Work with a partner to make a diagram of your classroom. Show measurements, such as the length of the walls, the board, and the desks. Include units for each measurement.

3 Research distances between planets and the sun in kilometers. Create a poster that shows the arrangement of planets and describes their distance from the sun in scientific notation.

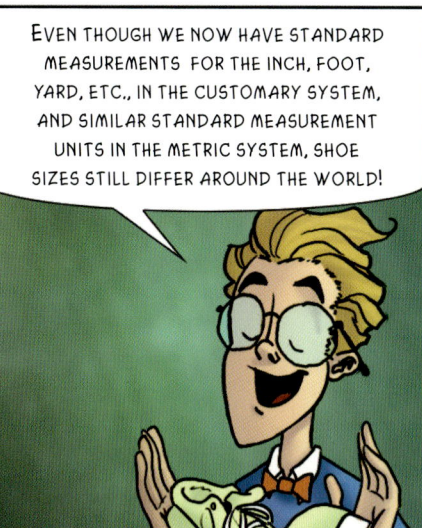

| CHAPTER 2 |

Mathematical Relationships

How can relationships between numbers be described and determined?

ESSENTIAL VOCABULARY
- decimal p. 23
- denominator p. 22
- fraction p. 22
- improper fraction p. 22
- mean p. 30
- median p. 30
- mode p. 30
- numerator p. 22
- percent p. 23
- proportion p. 25
- range p. 30
- rate p. 24
- ratio p. 24

We have ten digits and we use these digits to write numbers. If digits are the letters, then numbers are the words in the language of math and science. Just as we can use letters to make words and express thoughts, we can use numbers. We can calculate with numbers, and communicate with them. There are relationships between numbers that allow us to write them in different forms. A scientist can express data in different ways by using these different forms.

◀ Recent studies show that 66% of California's coastline is actively eroding. You can use a fraction, decimal, or percentage to express this number. You can also use rates to describe the amount of erosion per year.

$$66\% = 0.66 = \frac{2}{3}$$

Writing Numbers in Different Forms

There are three main ways to express numbers, whether they are whole numbers or parts of a whole. Whole numbers are numbers greater than or equal to one. Fractions, decimals, and percents are numbers that show parts of a whole. The great thing about numbers is that they can be expressed in any of these forms and converted from one to another.

Fractions

A **fraction** is a number that shows a part of a whole. Fractions are expressed with a **numerator**, or the quantity above the line of the fraction. Fractions also have a **denominator**, or the quantity below the line of the fraction. The denominator tells the number of equal parts in the whole. The numerator tells how many equal parts of the whole are being counted.

Five-eighths (5/8) is a fraction that shows 5 of 8 equal parts. Five-eighths is less than one. Eight-eighths (8/8) is equal to one. Fractions with a numerator larger than the denominator are called **improper fractions**. An improper fraction is greater than one. Nine-eighths (9/8) is an improper fraction. Nine-eighths (9/8) can also be written as the mixed number one and one-eighth (1 1/8).

MATHEMATICAL RELATIONSHIPS

Decimals

A **decimal** is another way to express a number that is not a whole number. The decimal system is based on units of ten. We can use decimals to show fractions. 0.1 is a decimal that is equal to 1/10. That means that 0.1 shows 1 of 10 equal parts. Decimals are used most often to express amounts of money. In science, decimals are used to show measurements.

Percents

A **percent** is a number that represents the number of parts out of 100. For example, ten percent (10%) is equal to 10 parts of 100 (10/100). In science, data results are often expressed in percents.

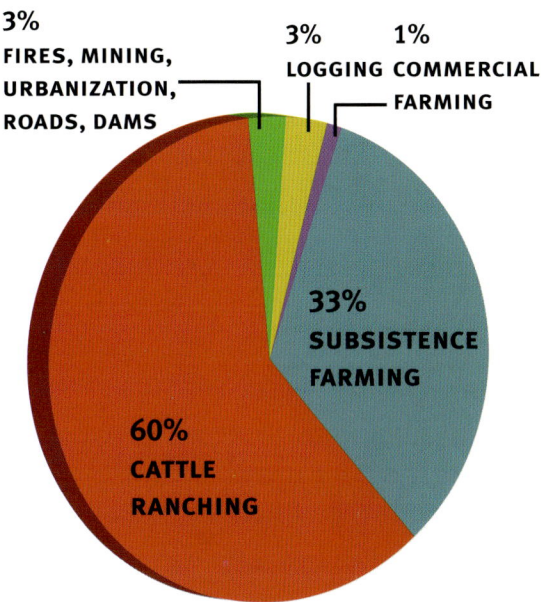

CURRENT CAUSES OF DEFORESTATION IN THE AMAZON

- 3% FIRES, MINING, URBANIZATION, ROADS, DAMS
- 3% LOGGING
- 1% COMMERCIAL FARMING
- 33% SUBSISTENCE FARMING
- 60% CATTLE RANCHING

▲ Data results are often expressed in percents.

▼ We can show equivalent amounts in the form of fractions, decimals, and percents.

$$\frac{1}{10} = \frac{10}{100} = 0.1 = 10\%$$

$$\frac{1}{4} = \frac{25}{100} = 0.25 = 25\%$$

$$\frac{1}{2} = \frac{50}{100} = 0.5 = 50\%$$

CHAPTER 2

Relationships Between Numbers

Suppose you are collecting data about the number of short-stemmed plants versus the number of long-stemmed plants in a sample. You will have to look at the relationship between the two numbers to analyze your results. There are different ways to examine the relationships between numbers.

Ratios

A **ratio** is the relationship between two quantities. A ratio is expressed as the quotient of one divided by the other. We can write the ratio of x to y as $x:y$, or x/y. So if there were 4 short-stemmed plants and 8 long-stemmed plants, the ratio between the numbers would be written as 4:8. This can be simplified to 1:2. For every 1 short-stemmed plant, there are 2 long-stemmed plants. Ratios are useful when analyzing data from surveys.

▼ A ratio is a good way to express relationships between quantities.

SCIENCE AND MATH
Ratios in Chemistry

In a compound you can find the ratio of combining atoms by looking at the subscripts in the chemical, or molecular, formula. The formula for water is H_2O. That means the ratio of hydrogen atoms to oxygen atoms is 2 to 1, 2:1, or 2/1.

Rates

A **rate** is a special type of ratio that presents two terms in different units. When food is sold at a certain price per pound, that is a rate. Science often uses unit rates to describe speed, such as millimeters per second, or kilometers per hour. The word *per* is often a signal word that a rate is being used. Rates can also be expressed as x/y.

▼ A rate is often used to show speed.

24

MATHEMATICAL RELATIONSHIPS

Proportions

A **proportion** is the relationship between two equal ratios. Proportions are often used when making models or maps. For example, if every centimeter on a map equals 5 actual kilometers, you have a 1:5 ratio. That means every 5 centimeters on the map will be equal to 25 kilometers, and so on. The proportion of the equal ratios can be expressed as an equation:

$$\frac{1}{5} = \frac{5}{25}$$

{ The Root of the Meaning: The word **PROPORTION** is based on the Latin word *proportio*, which means relationship of parts or analogy. An analogy is a comparison between two related things. }

If you are making a scaled model or diagram of an object, you can find the correct dimensions for each part by solving the proportion between the real object and the model. For example, suppose you were making a model of a human cell. The average diameter of a human cell is 0.01 cm and the diameter of your model cell is 100 cm. The ratio is 0.01:100. The average diameter of the nucleus in a human cell is 0.0005 cm. You can find diameter of the nucleus for your model by solving the proportion.

$$\frac{0.01}{100} = \frac{0.0005}{?}$$

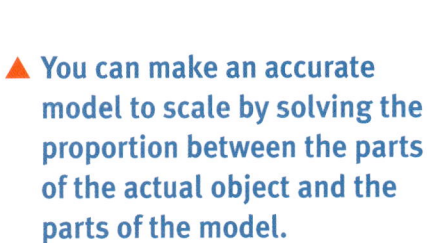

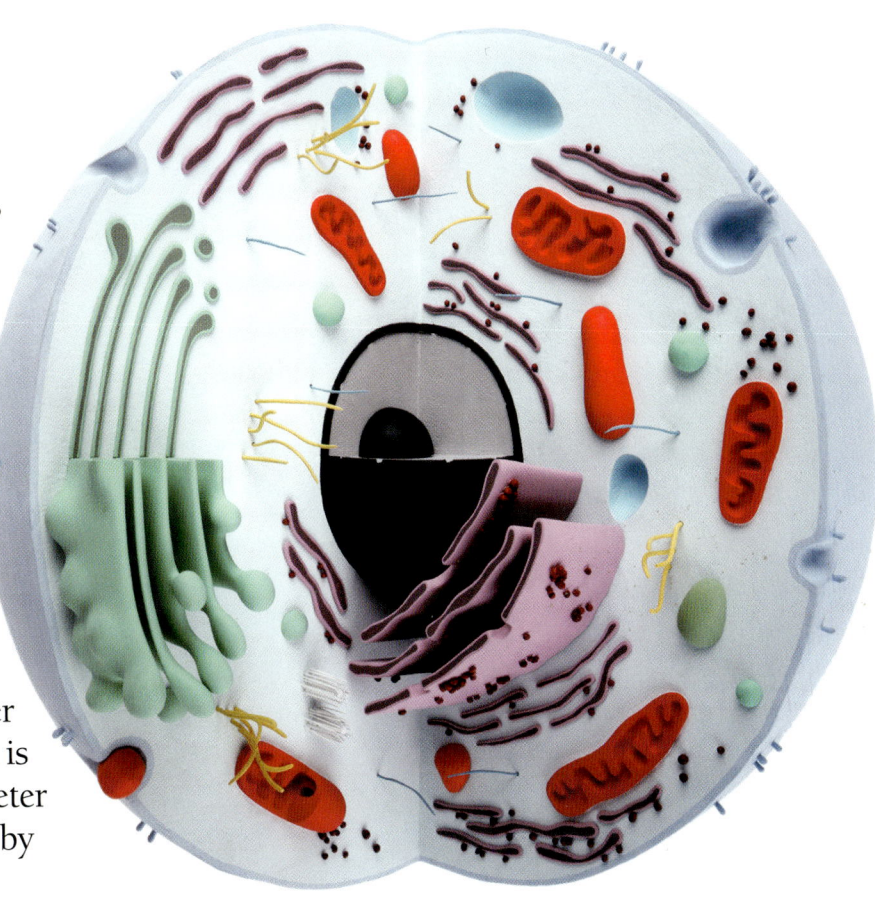

▲ You can make an accurate model to scale by solving the proportion between the parts of the actual object and the parts of the model.

25

Direct and Inverse Relationships

When analyzing scientific data, you may find that graphs can help you see the relationship between variables in your experiments. When a change in one variable results in a change in another variable in the same way, there is a direct relationship between the variables. We call this type of relationship a direct correlation. For example, if you increase the number of rotations on a wheel, the speed that the wheel travels across the ground will increase. That shows there is a direct relationship between the number of rotations of the wheel and the speed of the wheel.

In a similar way, there is a direct relationship between the number of plants and animals in an ecosystem. So an ecosystem with many plants will have many animals. An ecosystem with few plants will have few animals.

If data that represents a direct relationship is put on a line graph, you will see a positive slope. The plotted line would rise on the y-axis as it moves along the x-axis. In other words, the line would go from the bottom left to the top right of the graph.

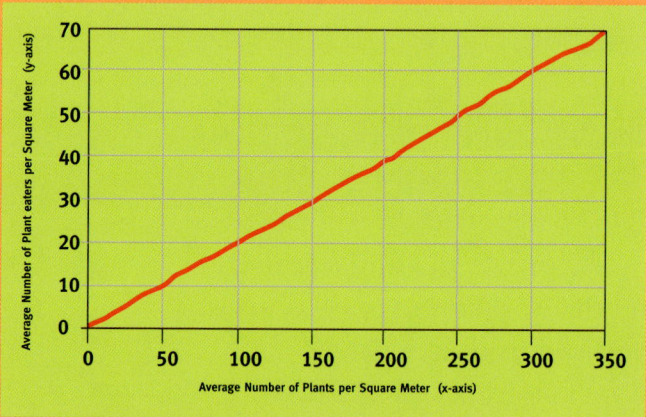

▲ There is a direct relationship between the number of plants and plant eaters in an ecosystem.

Mathematical Relationships

An indirect, or inverse, relationship is the opposite of a direct relationship. With an inverse relationship, the increase in one variable will result in a decrease in another variable. For example, the number of oil spills in the ocean has an inverse relationship to the number of animals in the ocean. The more oil spills, the fewer animals in the ocean. In a similar way, a decrease in temperatures in a region results in an increase in birds migrating. There is an inverse relationship between temperature and migration. We call this type of inverse relationship an indirect correlation.

If inverse relationships were represented in numbers and placed on a line graph, the slope of the line would be negative. That means that the line would fall along the y-axis as it moved along the x-axis. The line would slope from the top left of the graph down to the bottom right.

Checkpoint ✓

Visualize It

How can you use art to describe a direct and an inverse relationship? You might use a seesaw to see the concept more clearly. In an inverse relationship, when one side of the seesaw goes up, the other goes down. This is like the slope you might see on a line graph.

▼ There is an inverse relationship between the size of an oil spill and the population of seabirds in a region.

Chapter 2

Formulas

We use formulas to describe relationships between variables. There are formulas for finding just about any relationship in science. Formulas help us find the volume of a cube, a cylinder, or a prism. Formulas also allow us to find the area of a square, a rectangle, a circle, or a triangle. We can find the diameter and circumference of a circle with a formula. Speed, density, and force are represented in formulas used frequently in physical science. There are even formulas for converting temperature from Celsius units to Fahrenheit or kelvin.

We use letters to represent the variables in a formula. The letters in a formula represent something specific. Perhaps the most famous formula in science is Albert Einstein's mass–energy equivalence theory, or $E = mc^2$. In this formula, E represents energy, m means mass, and c is the speed of light in a vacuum. When the letters are replaced with the appropriate values for two of the three variables, the third one can be found.

Albert Einstein came up with one of the most famous mathematical formulas of all time, $E = mc^2$. ▶

MATHEMATICAL RELATIONSHIPS

To solve for one of the variables in a formula, you will need to know the values of the other variables in the formula. Then you may need to use algebraic concepts to isolate the unknown variable on one side of the equation. For example, the formula for the density of an object is Density = mass/volume. However, you may know the density and mass of an object but not the volume. You can plug the numbers you know into the equation and then solve for the variable that you do not know.

▼ The table below lists the formulas for relationships frequently explored in math and science.

Measurement	Relationship	Formula
area of a rectangle	Area = length x width	$A = l \times w$
area of a triangle	Area = 1/2 (base x height)	$A = (b \times h)/2$
density	density = mass/volume	$d = m/v$
volume of a rectangular prism	volume = length x width x height	$v = l \times w \times h$
speed	speed = distance/time	$S = d/t$
acceleration	acceleration = (final velocity – original velocity)/time	$A = (fv-ov)/t$
force	force = mass x acceleration	$F = m \times a$

SCIENCE AND MATH

Find the speed of an object that travels a total distance of 5 km in 15 minutes. Use the appropriate formula from the chart above.

Density = mass / volume

29

CHAPTER 2

Measures of Central Tendency

When you are faced with a series of numbers in a data set, there is a group of measures that can give useful information about the numbers. These are called measures of central tendency.

Mean

Another word for the **mean** of a set of numbers is the average. The mean is the sum of the numbers in a data set divided by the number of items in the data set. Let's say you have the following set of numbers: 17, 16, 21, 18, 18, 15, 12. The mean would be 16.7.

17 + 16 + 21 + 18 + 18 + 15 + 12 = 117/7 = (16.7)

Median

The **median** of a number set is the middle of the set. About half the numbers are above and half the numbers are below the median. You need to put the numbers in order to find the median. (For an even set of numbers, average the two middle numbers to find the median.) The median for this set is 17.

12 15 16 (17) 18 18 21

Mode

The most frequently occurring number in a set is the **mode**. It is useful to know the number that occurs most frequently in a set. Sometimes, the mode and the mean or median are the same number.
18 appears twice, so the mode is 18.

12 15 16 17 (18) (18) 21

▲ Measures of central tendency can be used on a wide variety of scientific data.

Range

The **range** in a data set is the difference between the lowest and highest numbers in the set. The range tells you how spread out the data is. The range of this set is 9.

12 15 16 17 18 18 21   21–12 = (9)

SCIENCE AND MATH

Look at the Celsius temperatures on the climograph below. Find the mean, median, mode, and range of the data:
–8°, –5°, –4°, 0°, 10°, 12°, 13°, 13°, 9°, 5°, –1°, –7°

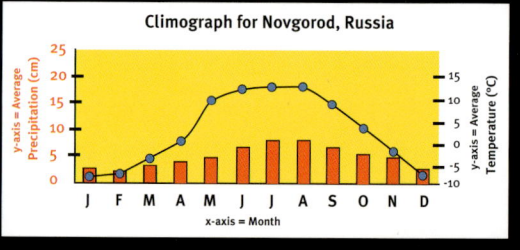

30

MATHEMATICAL RELATIONSHIPS

Summing Up

- We can use numbers to show different relationships between numbers.

- When we represent numbers as fractions, decimals, or percents, they can be converted back and forth easily to represent a part of a whole.

- Ratios, rates, and proportions also show how numbers can be related to one another.

- Direct and inverse relationships as well as formulas can show that numbers represent real data.

Putting It All Together

Choose from the research activities below. Work independently, in pairs, or in small groups. Then share your findings with the class.

1 Do a survey of the footwear worn by your class. Find what percent of students is wearing each type of shoe (sneakers, sandals, boots, or others). What do you notice about the sum of the percents?

2 Write a sentence explaining what a rate is. Then give a rate and tell what it describes. Indicate what an increase or decrease in the rate indicates. Compare your example with those of your classmates.

3 Find the amount of rainfall in your city or town each month last year. Round each amount to the nearest whole number. Then find the mean, median, mode, and range of the data. Suppose the greatest amount is doubled. How would this change affect the measures of central tendency?

31

| CHAPTER 3 |

Representing and Interpreting Data

How can data be organized and interpreted?

When conducting scientific experiments, it is extremely important that we display and interpret our data properly. It is the way we communicate the results of our work. Other scientists can then compare and contrast their own work with ours.

One of the best ways to show our work is through visual representation. Tables and graphs can be used to communicate something quickly and clearly that might otherwise take a very long time to explain with words alone. Graphic forms, such as tally charts and data tables, help us organize our information into formats that are easy to understand.

ESSENTIAL VOCABULARY
- bar graph p. 35
- circle graph p. 39
- histogram p. 38
- line graph p. 36
- scatter plot p. 40

CHAPTER 3

Data Tables

A data table is one of the simplest ways to represent data. It simply shows rows and columns with titles clearly labeled. The table itself must have a title to indicate what it represents. Units of measure are usually shown in parentheses.

Suppose you want to investigate how far a toy car will roll off a ramp. You decide to repeat the trial seven times to get a reliable data set to analyze. A data table is a useful tool for recording this information. Look at the data table to the right. The table has a title, and each column also has a title. The unit of measure is shown as well (meters). The data display makes it easy to compare the numbers in the set, to add more trials to the set, and to find measures of central tendency, such as the mean, mode, median, and range.

Distance Car Traveled From Ramp

Trial Number	Distance Traveled (meters)
Trial 1	14
Trial 2	17
Trial 3	12
Trial 4	15
Trial 5	14
Trial 6	16.5
Trial 7	12.5

▲ Data tables help us record results.

▼ Conversion tables help us to convert metric units to customary units, and vice versa.

Measurement Conversion Table

Quantity	Metric		Customary	
length		1 millimeter (mm)	0.039 inch (in)	
	10 millimeters (mm)	1 centimeter (cm)	0.39 inch (in)	0.033 foot (ft)
	100 centimeters (cm)	1 meter (m)	3.9 feet (ft)	1.094 yards (yd)
	1,000 meters (m)	1 kilometer (km)	1,093.6 yards (yd)	0.621 mile (mi)
mass	1,000 milligrams (mg)	1 gram (g)	n/a	n/a
	1,000 grams (g)	1 kilogram (kg)	n/a	n/a
weight	0.1019 kilogram (kg)	1 newton (N)	3.597 ounce (oz)	0.2248 pound (lb)
volume	1 cubic centimeter (cm^3)	1 milliliter (mL)	0.0338 fluid ounce (fl oz)	0.2 teaspoon (tsp)
	1,000 milliliters (mL)	1 liter (L)	1.0566 quarts (qt)	0.264 gallon (gal)
temperature		0° Celsius (°C)	32° Fahrenheit (°F)	
time		1 second (s)	1 second (s)	

Representing and Interpreting Data

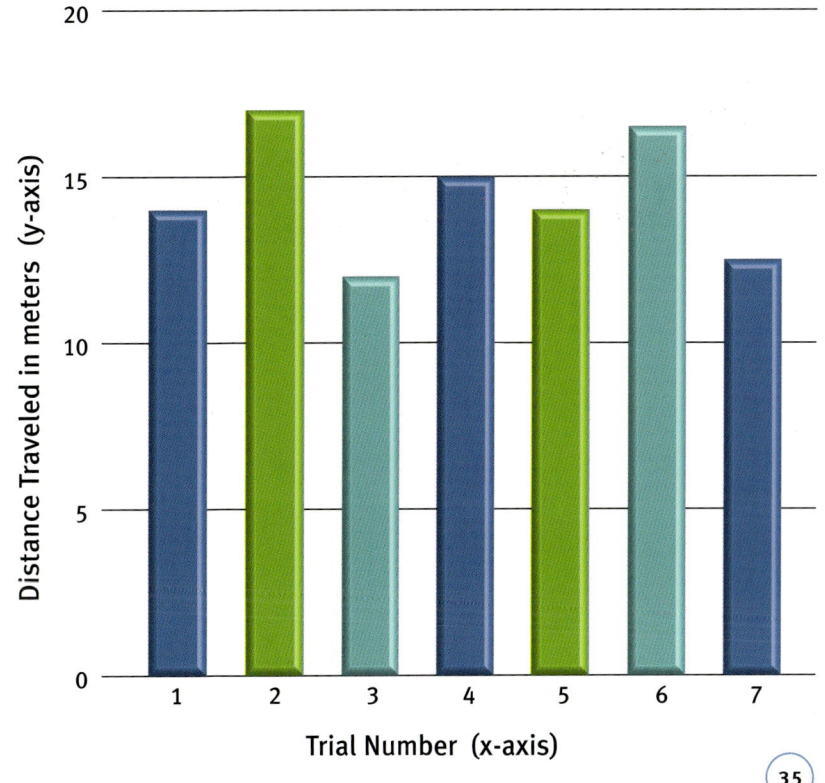

Bar Graphs

Once you collect your data in a table, you can display the information in the form of a bar graph. A **bar graph** is a diagram that represents number values by bars of different heights. The bottom of the graph, or the *x*-axis, represents the columns of the data table. The left side of the graph is the *y*-axis, which represents the rows of the data table. Compare the bar graph with the data table. Which is easier to read? Why do you think so?

Distance Car Traveled From Ramp

35

CHAPTER 3

Line Graphs

A **line graph** is a good way to represent data that changes over time. Like all other graphs, a line graph should have a descriptive title. The graph itself looks like a grid of boxes.

The grid is divided into an *x*-axis and a *y*-axis. The *x*-axis runs horizontally and has marks along it that represent equal periods of time. The *y*-axis runs vertically and represents the variable being changed. Data from a table can be displayed on a line graph. For example, the graph here shows the number of eggs laid by ducks at a local pond over the period of a year.

Sometimes more than one set of data can be graphed on the same line graph. You may be able to show the number of eggs laid by fish in the same pond over the same period. You could use a different color and provide a key to show which line stands for which set of data.

▼ The line graph shows data about when the ducks at this pond lay their eggs.

REPRESENTING AND INTERPRETING DATA

HANDS-ON SCIENCE
Make Your Own Graph

MATERIALS: graph paper, balloon, tape measure, felt-tip marker

1. Blow up the balloon and measure the circumference of the circle with a tape measure. Use a felt-tip marker to mark the exact part of the balloon that you measured. Record the measurement on a data table with the date.

2. The next day, measure the circumference of the balloon again. Record the measurement on the data table with the date.

3. Continue to measure the balloon circumference every day for five days.

4. Record your results on a line graph. Make the x-axis the number of days, and the y-axis the measurement of the balloon's circumference. What did your graph reveal about the balloon over time?

SCIENCE AND TECHNOLOGY

Graphing Calculators

A graphing calculator is a useful tool for scientists and mathematicians. It does more than just calculate equations. A graphing calculator can plot graphs and solve equations and at the same time graph the next point on a line. If you enter the parameters into the calculator, you can enter a value for the y-axis and one for the x-axis, and a formula will be solved with that plot point placed on the graph.

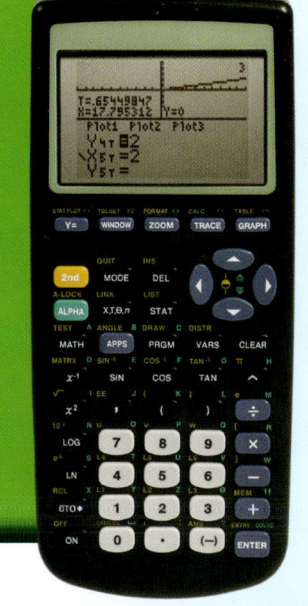

37

CHAPTER 3

Histogram

A **histogram** is a graph that shows how data are distributed in a set. A histogram may look like a bar graph at first, but the bottom of the graph represents a range of data and the side of the graph represents the frequency with which the data appear in the set. For example, you may do a study that involves the use of a large sampling of people. A histogram can quickly show you how many of your test subjects are in certain age groups. This kind of graph works best when you have a large set of data and would like to organize it in ranges.

Age Ranges of Test Subjects

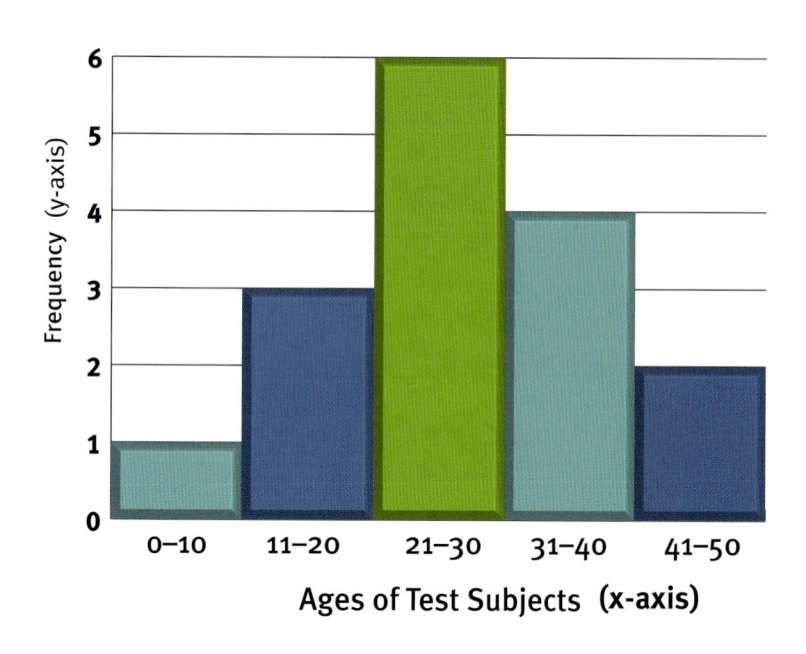

Frequency (y-axis)

Ages	Frequency
0–10	1
11–20	3
21–30	6
31–40	4
41–50	2

Ages of Test Subjects (x-axis)

Circle Graph

A **circle graph** is often called a pie chart. Similar to a real pie, a pie chart is divided into sections to represent parts of a whole. Circle graphs are often based on 100 percent, or a whole. Take a look at the circle graph on this page. It shows the percentages of different animal groups that make up an entire ecosystem.

Some circle graphs may record the total number of objects in a set, but the visual representation still shows the percent that each object is out of a whole. A circle graph is effective when one section of your data set represents a much larger percent than the rest. It quickly shows the viewer the significance of that part of the study.

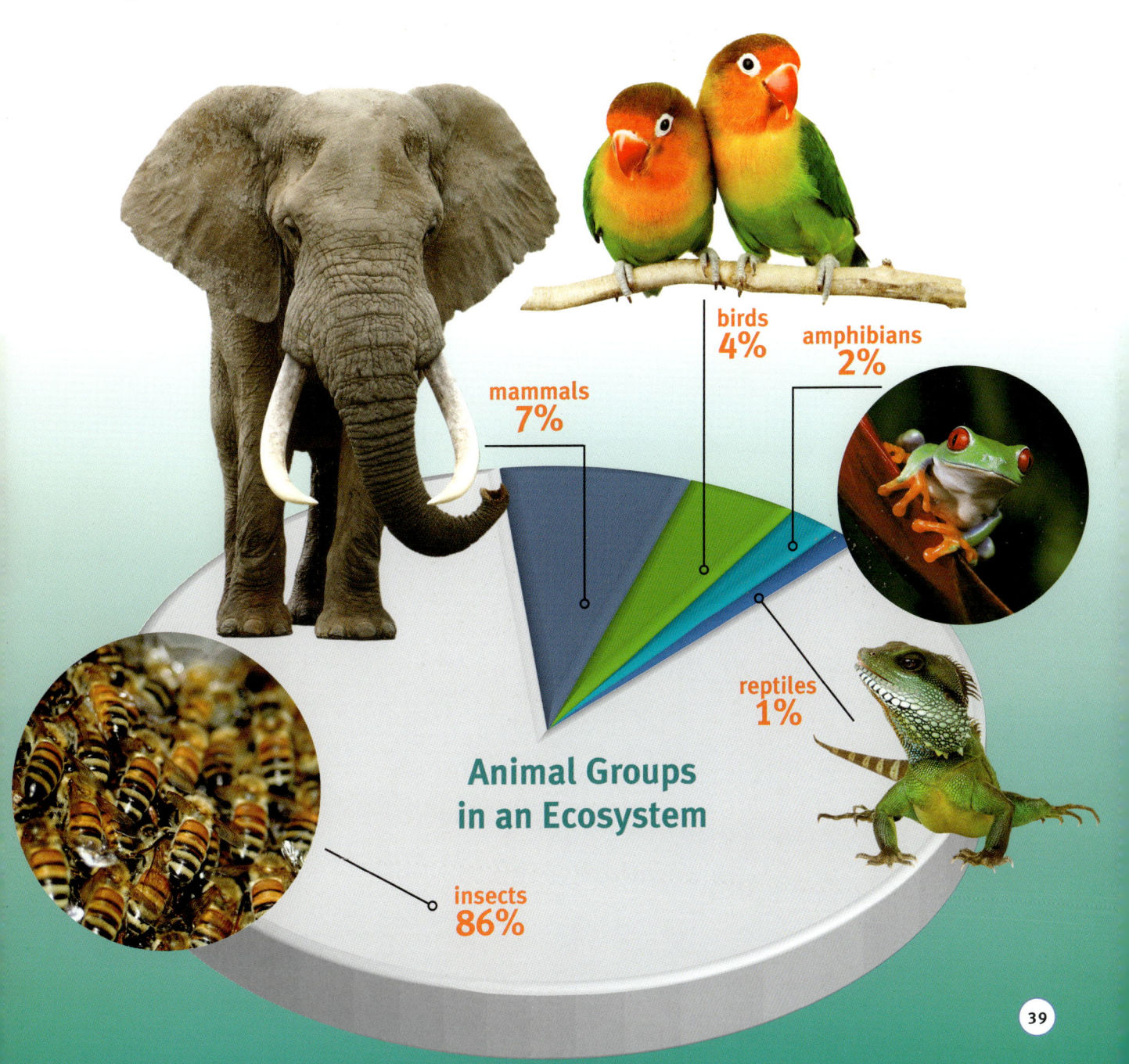

Animal Groups in an Ecosystem

- mammals 7%
- birds 4%
- amphibians 2%
- reptiles 1%
- insects 86%

Chapter 3

Scatter Plot

If the data you are collecting suggests a trend, you may find that a **scatter plot** is the best way to display and analyze the data. A scatter plot is similar to a line graph because it plots points on a graph with an *x*-axis and a *y*-axis. It shows the relationship between two variables. However, with a scatter plot, there are too many points to join with a line. These graphs are useful if you have a lot of data to display, such as the results of many data readings.

Note that a scatter plot diagram does not prove a cause-and-effect relationship. However, scatter plots that form a pattern do suggest the possibility of a cause-and-effect relationship. Analyzing the patterns on a scatter plot diagram shows that more studies should be done to clarify the relationship between the two variables. When using graphs to represent your data, you should think about the kind of data you are presenting and the most appropriate type of graph or chart for displaying the data. A carefully chosen graph will help people quickly understand and analyze your data.

Temperature and Plant Growth

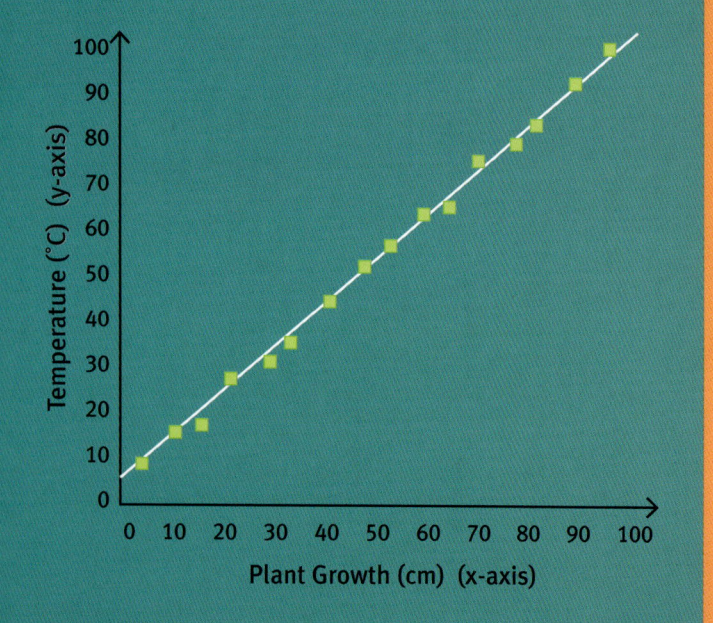

▲ This scatter plot suggests a direct, positive relationship between the temperature in an ecosystem and the growth of plants.

Temperature and Animal Growth

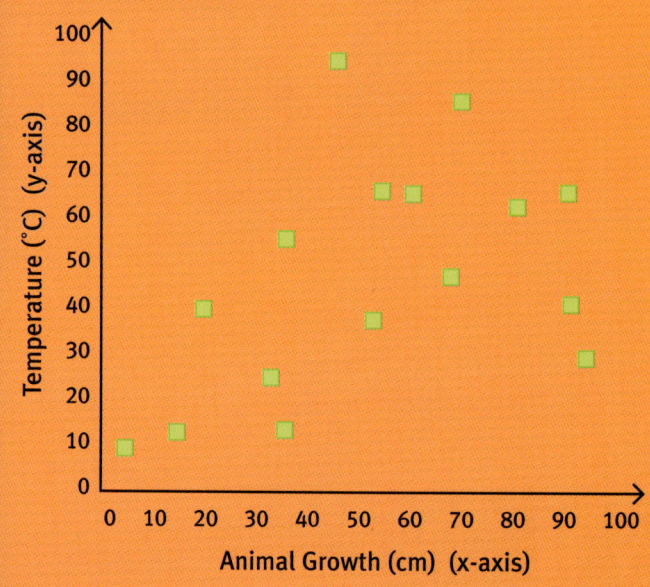

▲ This scatter plot suggests that there is no relationship between the temperature of an ecosystem and the growth of the animals in that ecosystem.

REPRESENTING AND INTERPRETING DATA

Summing Up

- Putting your data in a visual form is an important part of presenting it to others and analyzing it.

- Graphs can suggest trends in data and tell others where more study is needed.

- The types of graphs that scientists use include data tables, bar graphs, line graphs, histograms, circle graphs, and scatter plots.

Putting It All Together

Choose from the research activities below. Work independently, in pairs, or in small groups. Then share your findings with the class.

1 Find a bar graph in a newspaper or magazine. Attach the graph to a sheet of poster board. Present the graph to the class, identifying the information that is presented.

2 Keep track of the highest temperature where you live every day for one week in a data table. Work with a partner to create a line graph to display the data. Present your data table and line graph to the class. Describe any trends you see in the data.

3 Think of a question you can use to survey your class. For example, you might ask about favorite foods, favorite types of movies, or number of pets. In a small group, conduct your survey. Record the results in a data table. Then display the data in a circle graph.

| CONCLUSION |

The World of Mathematics and Science Grows

How do you picture the future? Do you imagine people living in space or zipping between planets for a night out? Or maybe you picture people learning to live on Earth without making waste or destroying habitats. However you envision the future, it's math and science that will get us there. After all, math and science got us to where we are today. They are behind the video games, airplanes, and modern medicines that are part of our everyday lives.

In the same way, the treasures of the future will also depend on math and science. Scientists around the world will experiment, invent, and discover new things using the language of mathematics. They will communicate their discoveries to the rest of us using the language of mathematics. Together, math and science will help us make connections that will lead to new answers, new solutions, and discoveries. What big changes do you think math and science will bring in the future?

This building could not be built without the language of math and science.

HOW TO WRITE AN
Objective Argument

Scientists often have to use the data from their studies to make an argument about the topic they are studying. Suppose a scientist has been studying the rain forest over a long period of time. She notices the impact that human activity has had on the ecosystem. She uses the data she has collected about the impact of human activity to support her argument that people should lessen their activity in the rain forest.

She might choose to publish her argument in a scientific journal, or in a newspaper or magazine, with the hope that the public will pay attention to this important scientific issue.

Like this scientist, you should begin your scientific argument with a clear statement of the point being made or the hypothesis being explored. The hypothesis statement should be simple and state what you are setting out to prove in your paper. The arguments you make should then be supported with measurable data and research. The more mathematical data you can present in a scientific paper or argument, the more convincing your argument will be.

Whether your argument will be read by only your science teacher or by thousands of people in the scientific community, the data and graphs you include in your paper should be clear, concise, and able to be proven through repeated experimentation or duplicated research.

1. **Choose a topic that interests you.**

2. **Gather information.**

3. **Write your argument.**
   - Present your idea.
   - State what you predict might happen if your idea is correct.
   - Present evidence/data in graphs and charts and describe how the evidence supports or contradicts your predictions.
   - Make a conclusion and propose a possible solution.

4. **Edit and revise your argument.**
   - Be careful not to give your opinion.
   - Readers will take your argument more seriously if you remain objective.
   - Be sure to carefully proofread for errors.

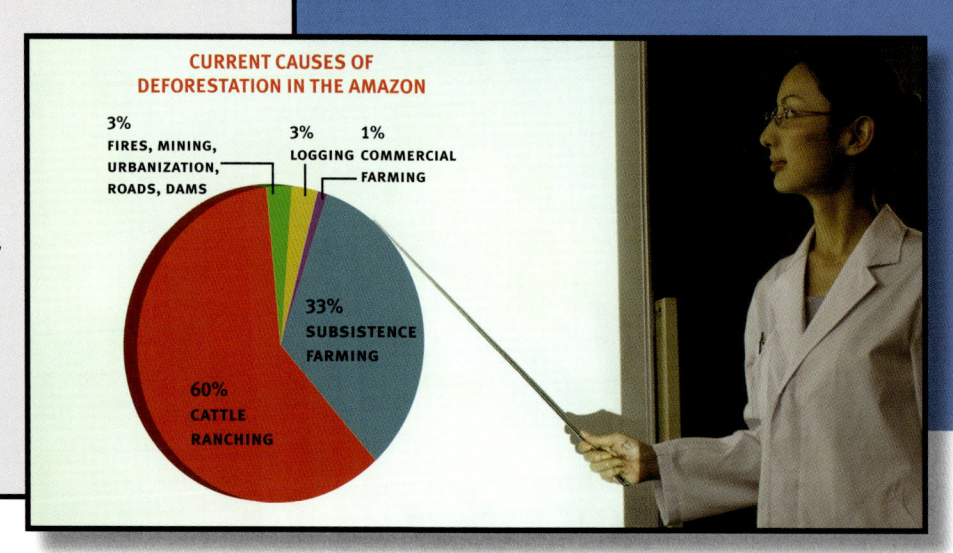

CURRENT CAUSES OF DEFORESTATION IN THE AMAZON

- 3% FIRES, MINING, URBANIZATION, ROADS, DAMS
- 3% LOGGING
- 1% COMMERCIAL FARMING
- 33% SUBSISTENCE FARMING
- 60% CATTLE RANCHING

Sample Argument

The Amazon rain forest is home to more plant and animal species than anywhere else on Earth. It is also one of the world's greatest natural resources. About 20% of Earth's oxygen is produced by the Amazon rain forest. For this reason it is often called the "Lungs of our Planet." Today, 121 prescription drugs sold around the world come from plant-derived sources. Although 25% of all drugs are derived from rain forest ingredients, scientists have tested only 1% of tropical plants. Time is running out.

Today, more than 20% of the Amazon rain forest has been destroyed by human impact. The land is being cleared for ranching, mining, logging, and farming. More than half of the world's rain forests have been destroyed by fire and logging in the last 50 years. More than 200,000 acres are burned every day around the world, or over 150 acres every minute. Experts also estimate that 130 species of plants, animals, and insects are lost every day. At the current rate of destruction, it is estimated that the last remaining rain forests could be destroyed in less than 40 years.

We must work closely with other nations to reduce the level of slashing and burning. We can offer new ideas about sustainable forestry. We can also help these governments to create incentives for foreign investment such as pharmaceutical companies. Together, we can help these nations protect their own interests, and ours, by preserving this invaluable habitat, and our planet.

Glossary

bar graph — (BAR GRAF) *noun* a diagram that represents number values by bars of different heights (page 35)

circle graph — (SER-kul GRAF) *noun* a diagram divided into parts that represent proportions of the whole (page 39)

customary system — (KUS-tuh-mair-ee SIS-tem) *noun* a system of measurement that includes ounces, pounds, cups, and gallons (page 8)

decimal — (DEH-sih-mul) *noun* a fraction with a denominator of 10, or a multiple of 10 such as 100 or 1,000 (page 23)

denominator — (dih-NAH-mih-nay-ter) *noun* the number below the line in a fraction; shows the number of equal parts into which the whole is divided (page 22)

dimensional analysis — (dih-MEN-shuh-nul uh-NA-lih-sis) *noun* the practice of expressing units that show the same relations (page 13)

estimate — (ES-tih-mit) *noun* a rough calculation that is not exact (page 16)

exponent — (EK-spoh-nent) *noun* a smaller number that is placed after and above another number to show how many times that number is to be multiplied by itself (page 14)

formula — (FOR-myuh-luh) *noun* a mathematical rule or relationship that is expressed in symbols (page 12)

fraction — (FRAK-shun) *noun* a number that is a part of a whole (page 22)

histogram — (HIS-tuh-gram) *noun* a graph that shows how data is distributed in a set (page 38)

improper fraction — (im-PRAH-per FRAK-shun) *noun* a fraction with a numerator larger than the denominator (page 22)

line graph — (LINE GRAF) *noun* a diagram that represents the relationship between two variables (page 36)

mean	(MEEN) *noun* the sum of the numbers in a data set divided by the number of items in the data set (page 30)
median	(MEE-dee-un) *noun* the middle number in a data set (page 30)
metric system	(MEH-trik SIS-tem) *noun* a standardized system of measurements based on the number 10 (page 9)
mode	(MODE) *noun* the most frequently occurring number in a data set (page 30)
numerator	(NOO-muh-ray-ter) *noun* the number above the line in a fraction; shows how many parts of the denominator are taken (page 22)
percent	(per-SENT) *noun* the number of parts in every 100 (page 23)
proportion	(pruh-POR-shun) *noun* a relationship between two ratios (page 25)
range	(RANJE) *noun* the difference between the lowest and highest numbers in a set (page 30)
rate	(RATE) *noun* a type of ratio that presents two terms in different units (page 24)
ratio	(RAY-shee-oh) *noun* a relationship between two quantities that is expressed as the quotient of one divided by the other (page 24)
scatter plot	(SKA-ter PLAHT) *noun* a diagram that shows two variables that may or may not suggest a relationship between them (page 40)
scientific notation	(sy-en-TIH-fik noh-TAY-shun) *noun* a way of writing numbers in a decimal form by using exponents (page 14)

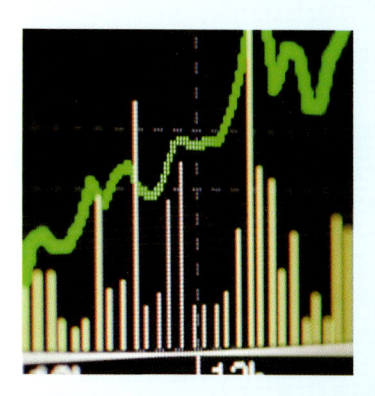

Index

bar graph, 35, 38, 41
circle graph, 39, 41
customary system, 8, 13, 17, 19
decimal, 9, 14–15, 22–23, 31
denominator, 22
density, 12, 17, 28–29
dimensional analysis, 13
estimate, 16–17
exponent, 14
formula, 12, 17, 28–29, 31, 37
fraction, 22–23, 31
histogram, 38, 41
improper fraction, 22
International System of Units (SI), 9, 11, 13, 17, 19
length, 8–9, 11–13, 17–19
line graph, 26–27, 36, 40–41
mass, 9, 11–13, 17, 28–29

mean, 30, 34
median, 30, 34
metric system, 9, 11, 13, 17, 19
mixed number, 22
mode, 30, 34
numerator, 22
percent, 22–23, 31, 39
proportion, 25, 31, 42
qualitative data, 6
quantitative data, 6
range, 30, 34, 38
rate, 24–25, 31
ratio, 24–25, 31
scatter plot, 40–41
scientific notation, 14–15
speed, 5, 12, 16–17, 26, 28
time, 4, 9, 12–13, 17, 36–37, 44
volume, 8–9, 11–13, 17, 28–29